ERIC CLAPTON FOR UKULELE

Cover photo: Getty Images / Rob Verhorst / Contributor

ISBN 978-1-5400-2823-5

For all works contained herein:
Unauthorized copying, arranging, adapting, recording, Internet posting, public performance,
or other distribution of the music in this publication is an infringement of copyright.
Infringers are liable under the law.

Visit Hal Leonard Online at
www.halleonard.com

Contact us:
Hal Leonard
7777 West Bluemound Road
Milwaukee, WI 53213
Email: info@halleonard.com

In Europe, contact:
Hal Leonard Europe Limited
42 Wigmore Street
Marylebone, London, W1U 2RN
Email: info@halleonardeurope.com

In Australia, contact:
Hal Leonard Australia Pty. Ltd.
4 Lentara Court
Cheltenham, Victoria, 3192 Australia
Email: info@halleonard.com.au

After Midnight

Words and Music by J. J. Cale

Copyright © 1970 Mijac Music and Warner-Tamerlane Publishing Corp.
Copyright Renewed
All Rights on behalf of Mijac Music Administered by
Sony/ATV Music Publishing LLC, 424 Church Street, Suite 1200, Nashville, TN 37219
International Copyright Secured   All Rights Reserved

Badge

Words and Music by Eric Clapton and George Harrison

First note

Verse
Moderately

1. Think-in' 'bout the times you drove _ in my car. ____
2. I told you not to wan-der 'round _ in the dark. ____
3. Talk-in' 'bout a girl that looks _ quite like you. ____

Think-in' that I might have drove _ you too far. ____
I told you 'bout the swans, that they live in the park. __
She did-n't have the time to wait _ in the queue. _

And I'm think-in' 'bout the
Then I told you 'bout the
She cried a-way her

To Coda ⊕ | 1.

love that you laid on my ta - ble.
kid. Now he's mar-ried to Ma-bel.
life since she fell out the cra - dle.

Copyright © 1969 by E.C. Music Ltd. and Harrisongs Ltd.
Copyright Renewed
International Copyright Secured All Rights Reserved

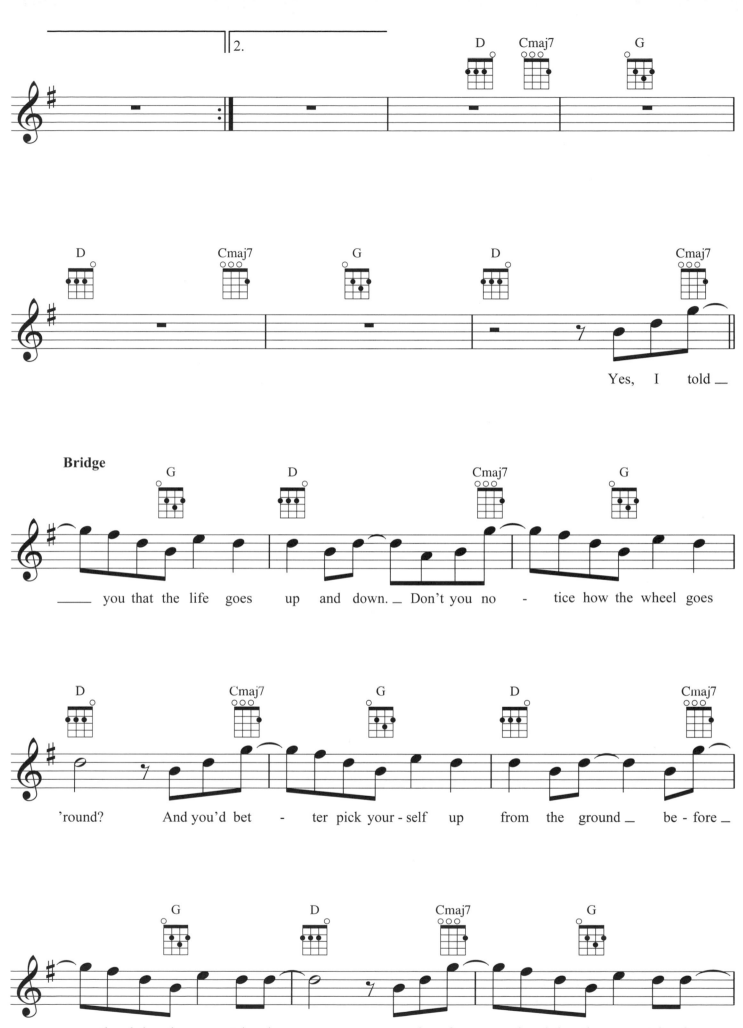

Yes, I told __

Bridge

__ you that the life goes up and down. __ Don't you no - tice how the wheel goes

'round? And you'd bet - ter pick your - self up from the ground __ be - fore __

__ they bring the cur - tain down, __ yes, be - fore __ they bring the cur - tain down. __

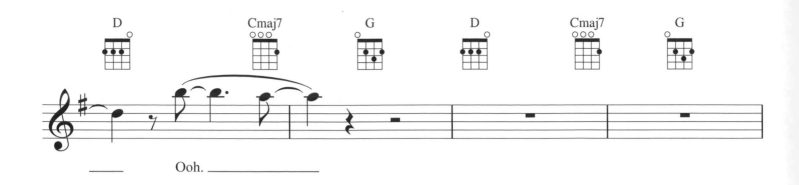

_____ Ooh. _____

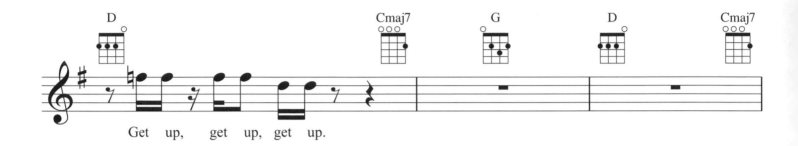

Get up, get up, get up.

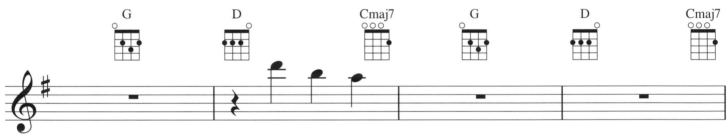

Yeah yeah yeah.

Yeah ____ yeah   yeah. __

D.C. al Coda

Coda

Bell Bottom Blues

Words and Music by Eric Clapton

First note
×××

Slow Rock beat

Verse
C   E

1. Bell   Bot - tom   Blues,   you   made   me
(2.) wrong,   but   it's   all
(3.) Blues,   don't   say   good -

Am   C   F   G

cry. ___   I don't want to   lose __ this feel - in'.
right, ___   the way that you   treat __ me, ba - by.
bye. ___   I'm sure we're gon - na   meet __ a - gain. ____

F   C   G7   C   E

If   I   could   choose __   a place   to
Once   I   was   strong, __   but   I   lost   the
And if we   do, _____   don't ya be sur -

Am   C   F   G

die, ___   it would be in _____ your __ arms. ___
fight. __   You won't find a   bet - ter __ los - er. }
prised __   if you find me with an - oth - er __ lov - er. }

Copyright © 1970, 1971, 1978 by Eric Patrick Clapton
Copyright Renewed
International Copyright Secured All Rights Reserved

Change the World

Words and Music by Wayne Kirkpatrick, Gordon Kennedy and Tommy Sims

Copyright © 1996 Downtown DMP Songs, Universal - PolyGram International Publishing, Inc., Sondance Kid Music,
Universal Music Corp., Universal Music - Brentwood Benson Publishing and Universal Music - Brentwood Benson Songs
All Rights for Downtown DMP Songs Administered by Downtown Music Publishing, LLC
All Rights for Sondance Kid Music Controlled and Administered by Universal - PolyGram International Publishing, Inc.
All Rights for Universal Music - Brentwood Benson Publishing and Universal Music - Brentwood Benson Songs Admin. at CapitolCMGPublishing.com
International Copyright Secured   All Rights Reserved

then ____ this love I have ____ in - side
And ____ our love will ____ rule _____ in ____ this

is ev - 'ry - thing it ____ seems. _____
king - dom we have ____ made. _____

But ____ for now I find _____
'Til then I'd be a fool _____

's on - ly in my ____ dreams ____ } that I can
wish - ing for the ____ day _____ }

Chorus

change _____ the world. ____

I would be ____ the sun - light in your u - ni - verse. ____

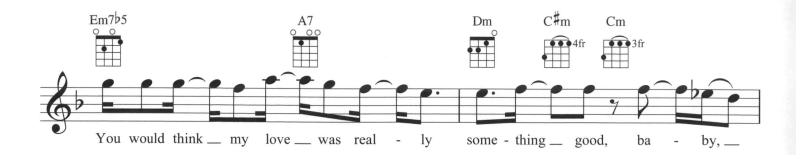

You would think — my love — was real - ly some - thing — good, ba - by, —

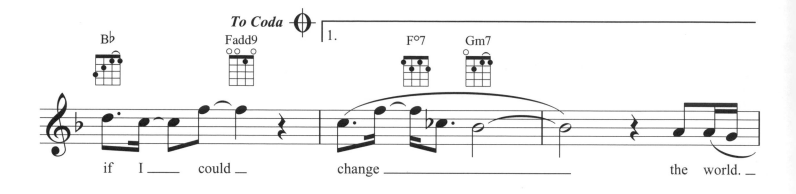

if I ___ could ___ change _____ the world. —

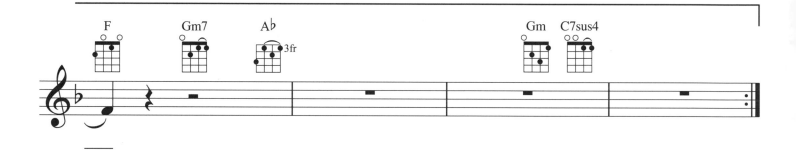

change _____ the world, _____ ba - by, —

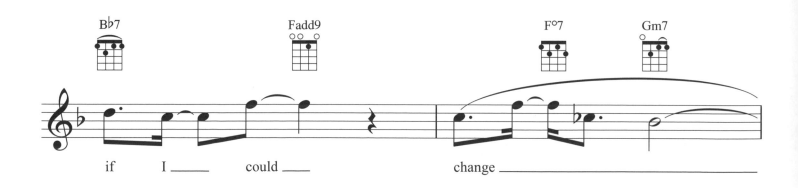

if I ___ could ___ change _____

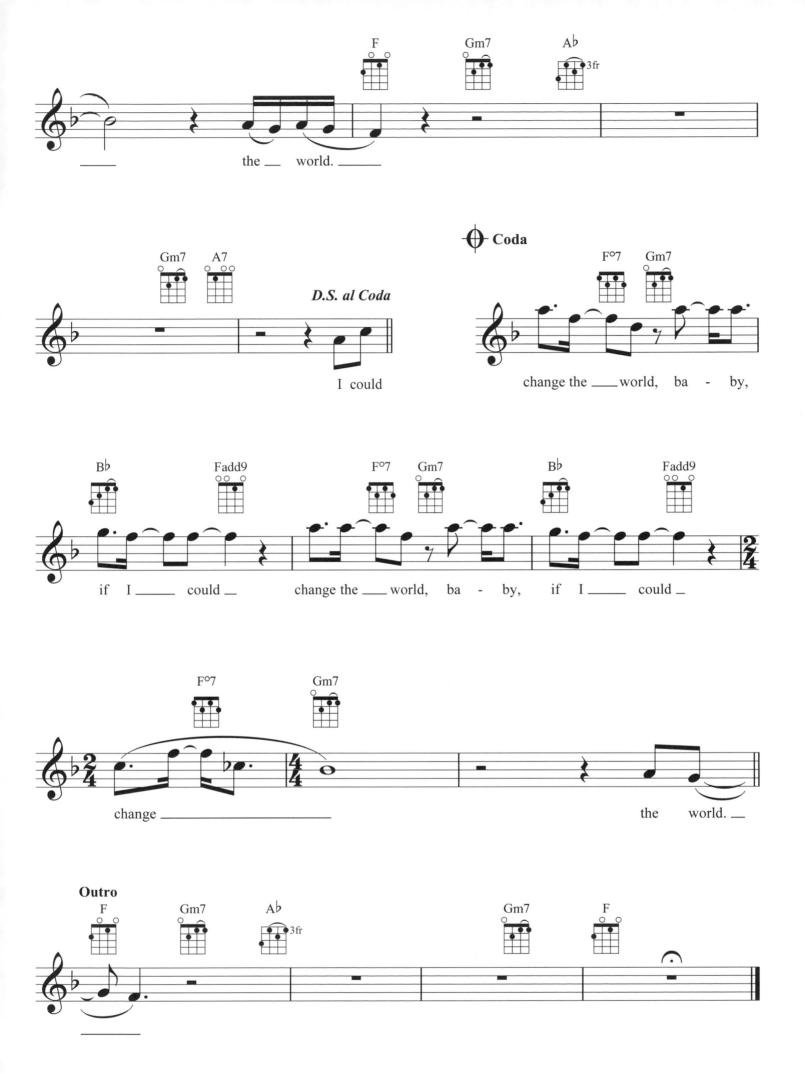

Cocaine
Words and Music by J.J. Cale

Copyright © 1975 Audigram Music
Copyright Renewed
All Rights Administered by BMG Rights Management (US) LLC
All Rights Reserved   Used by Permission

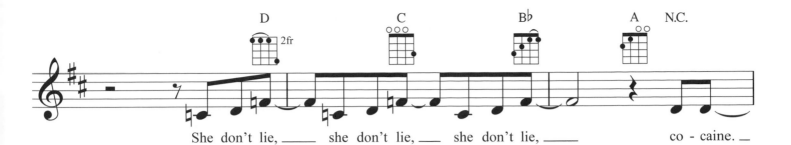

She don't lie, _____ she don't lie, _____ she don't lie, _____ co - caine. _____

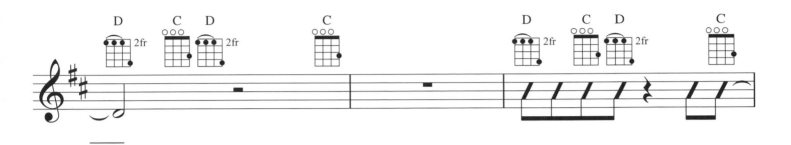

_____

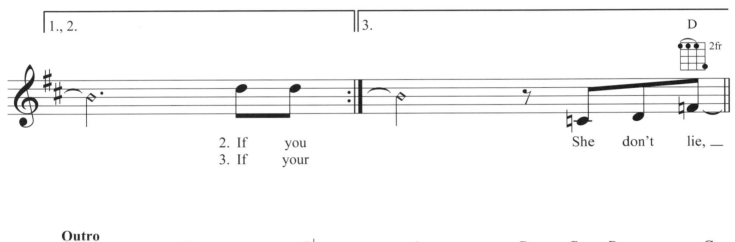

2. If you
3. If your

She don't lie, __

Outro

_____ she don't lie, _____ she don't lie, _____ co - caine. _____

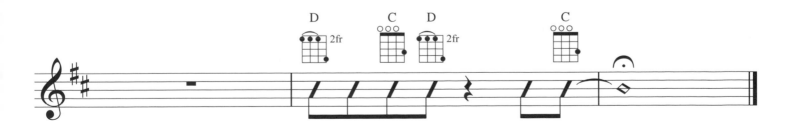

Forever Man

Words and Music by Jerry Lynn Williams

Copyright © 1976, 1985 UNIVERSAL - SONGS OF POLYGRAM INTERNATIONAL, INC. and
STAGE THREE MUSIC (CATALOGUES) LIMITED
Copyright Renewed
All Rights for STAGE THREE MUSIC (CATALOGUES) LIMITED Administered by STAGE THREE MUSIC (US) INC.,
A BMG CHRYSALIS COMPANY
All Rights Reserved   Used by Permission

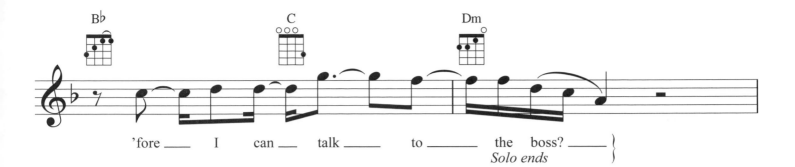

'fore ___ I can ___ talk ___ to ___ the boss? ___
Solo ends

(Instrumental)

Verse

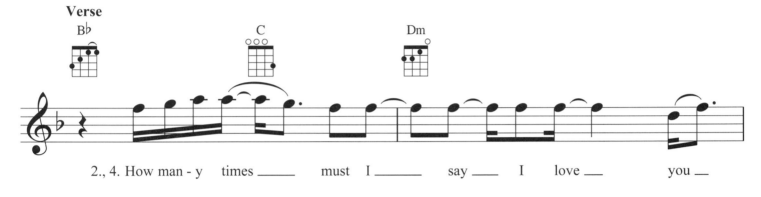

2., 4. How man - y times ___ must I ___ say ___ I love ___ you ___

be - fore you fi - n'ly un - der - stand? ___

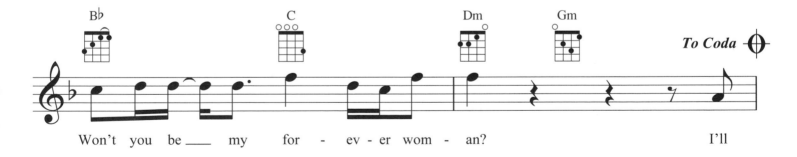

To Coda ⊕

Won't you be ___ my for - ev - er wom - an? ___ I'll

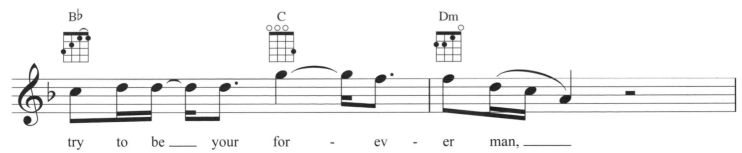

try to be ___ your for - ev - er man, ___

try   to   be ___ your   for - ev - er   man. _____

D.C. al Coda

(Instrumental)

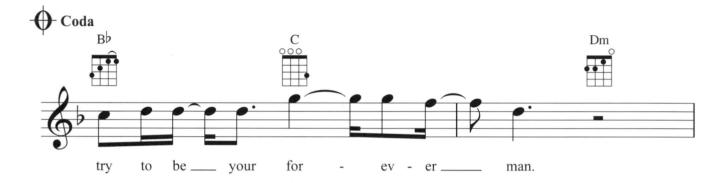

Coda

try   to   be ___ your   for - ev - er ___ man.

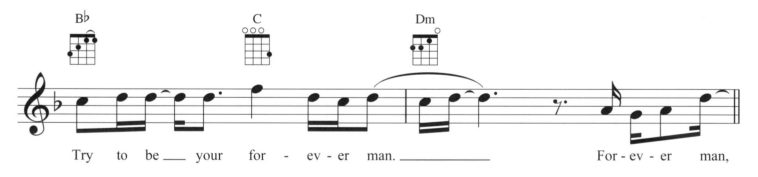

Try   to   be ___ your   for - ev - er   man. _____   For - ev - er   man,

Outro 1

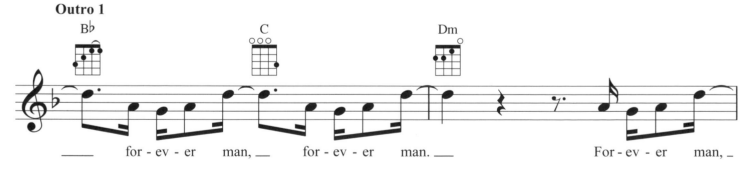

___ for - ev - er   man, ___ for - ev - er   man. ___   For - ev - er   man, _

___ for - ev - er   man, ___ for - ev - er _____ man.

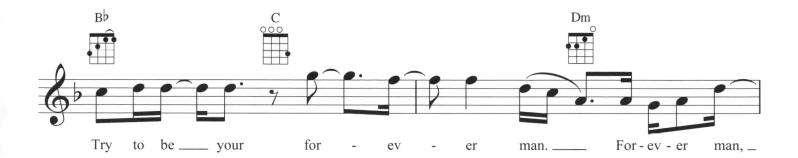

Try to be ___ your for - ev - er man. ___ For - ev - er man, ___

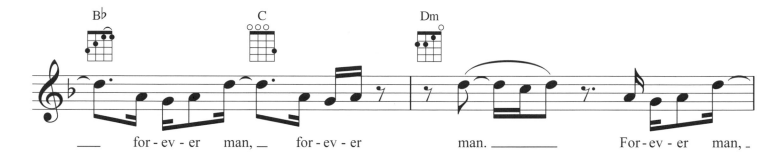

___ for - ev - er man, ___ for - ev - er man. ___ For - ev - er man, ___

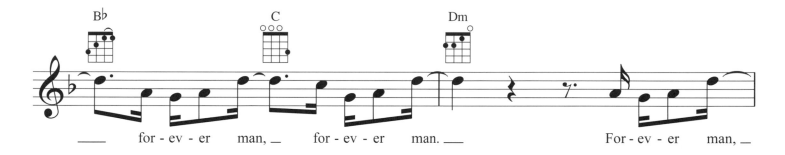

___ for - ev - er man, ___ for - ev - er man. ___ For - ev - er man, ___

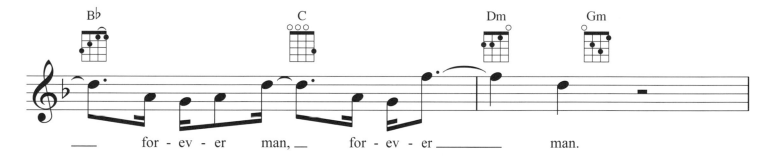

___ for - ev - er man, ___ for - ev - er ___ man.

Outro 2

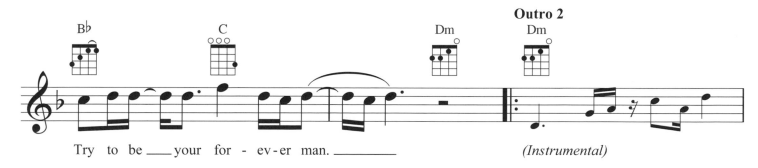

Try to be ___ your for - ev - er man. ___ *(Instrumental)*

Repeat ad lib. and fade

I Shot the Sheriff

Words and Music by Bob Marley

1. I shot the sher - iff, but I did not shoot the
2.–5. *See additional lyrics*

dep - u - ty. I shot the sher - iff,

but I did - n't shoot the dep - u - ty.

All a - round in my home town, they're try - ing to track me down. ___

___ They say they want to bring me in guilt - y for the

Copyright © 1974 Fifty-Six Hope Road Music Ltd. and Odnil Music Ltd.
Copyright Renewed
All Rights in North America Administered by Blue Mountain Music Ltd./Irish Town Songs (ASCAP)
and throughout the rest of the world by Blue Mountain Music Ltd. (PRS)
All Rights Reserved

Additional Lyrics

2. I shot the sheriff, but I swear it was in self-defense.
   I shot the sheriff, and they say it is a capital offense.
   Sheriff John Brown always hated me; for what, I don't know.
   Every time that I plant a seed, he said, "Kill it before it grows."
   He said, "Kill it before it grows." But I say:

3. I shot the sheriff, but I swear it was in self-defense.
   I shot the sheriff, but I swear it was in self-defense.
   Freedom came my way one day, and I started out of town.
   All of a sudden, I see Sheriff John Brown aiming to shoot me down.
   So I shot, I shot him down. But I say:

4. I shot the sheriff, but I did not shoot the deputy.
   I shot the sheriff, but I did not shoot the deputy.
   Reflexes got the better of me, and what is to be must be.
   Every day, the bucket goes to the well, but one day the bottom will drop out.
   Yes, one day the bottom will drop out. But I say:

5. I shot the sheriff, but I didn't shoot the deputy.
   I shot the sheriff, but I did not shoot no deputy.
   Instrumental fade

It's in the Way That You Use It

Words and Music by Eric Clapton and Robbie Robertson

Copyright © 1986 by E.C. Music Ltd.
International Copyright Secured   All Rights Reserved

So, don't you ev - er a - buse ___ it,

To Coda

don't let it go. _____ 1. No - bod - y's right ___

Verse

___ 'til some - bod - y's wrong. ___ No - bod - y's weak ___

___ 'til some - bod - y's strong. ___ No one gets luck -

- y 'til luck comes a - long. ___ No - bod - y's lone -

- ly 'til some - bod - y's gone. ___ It's in the way that you use ___

Knockin' on Heaven's Door

Words and Music by Bob Dylan

Copyright © 1973, 1976 Ram's Horn Music
International Copyright Secured   All Rights Reserved
Used by Permission

Knock, knock, knock-in' on heav-en's door. ___

(1., 3.) Knock, knock, knock-in' on heav-en's door. ___
(2.) *Guitar solo ad lib.*

Knock, knock, knock-in' on heav-en's door. ___

Interlude

To Coda

Ooh, ___ ooh. ___
(Solo continues)

Ooh, ___

*D.C. al Coda
(no repeat)*

Coda

ooh. ___ *(Solo ends)*

Lay Down Sally

Words and Music by Eric Clapton, Marcy Levy and George Terry

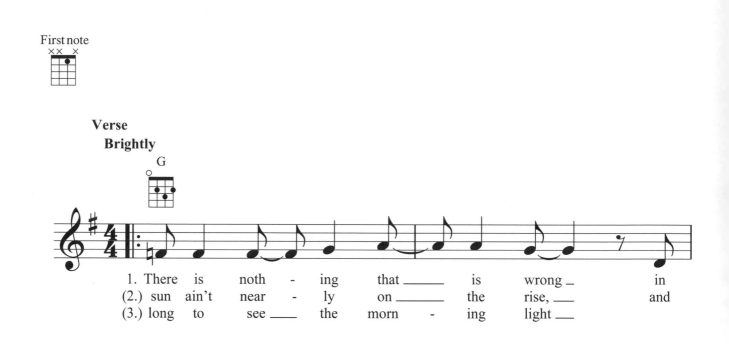

Copyright © 1977 by Eric Patrick Clapton and Throat Music Ltd.
Copyright Renewed
All Rights for Throat Music Ltd. Administered by Unichappell Music Inc.
International Copyright Secured   All Rights Reserved

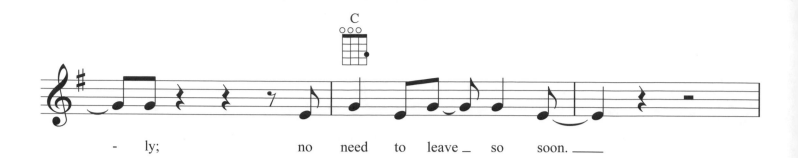

-ly;   no need to leave __ so soon. ____

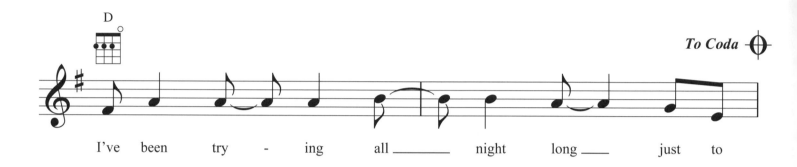

I've been try - ing all _____ night long ____ just to

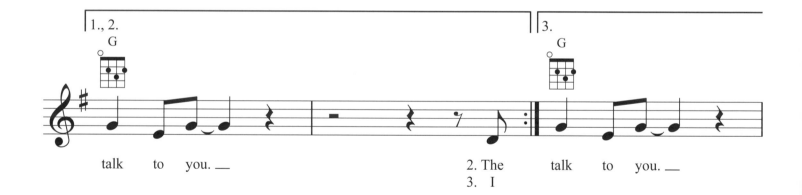

1., 2.   talk to you. __   2. The   3.   talk to you. __
                                                                   3. I

Coda

talk to you. __

Tears in Heaven

Words and Music by Eric Clapton and Will Jennings

First note

Verse
Moderate, relaxed tempo

1. Would you know my name _____
2. Would you hold my hand _____
3. Would you know my name _____

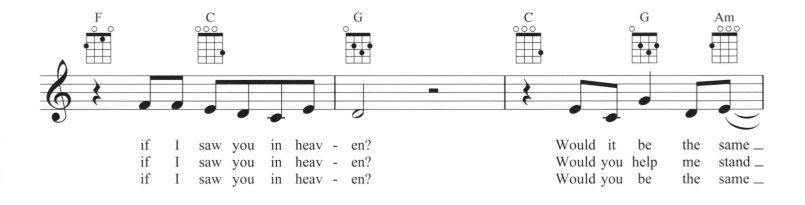

if I saw you in heav - en?   Would it be the same ___
if I saw you in heav - en?   Would you help me stand ___
if I saw you in heav - en?   Would you be the same ___

_____   if I saw you in heav - en?
_____   if I saw you in heav - en?
_____   if I saw you in heav - en?

Copyright © 1992 by E.C. Music Ltd. and Blue Sky Rider Songs
All Rights for Blue Sky Rider Songs Administered by Irving Music, Inc.
International Copyright Secured   All Rights Reserved

Chorus

(1., 3.) I must be strong ___ and car - ry on ___
(2.) I'll find my way ___ through night and day ___

___ 'cause I know ___ I don't be - long ___ here in heav-
___ 'cause I know ___ I just can't stay ___ here in heav-

To Coda

en.
en.

Bridge

Time can bring you down, ___ time can bend your knees. ___

Time can break the heart, ___ have you beg - gin' please, ___

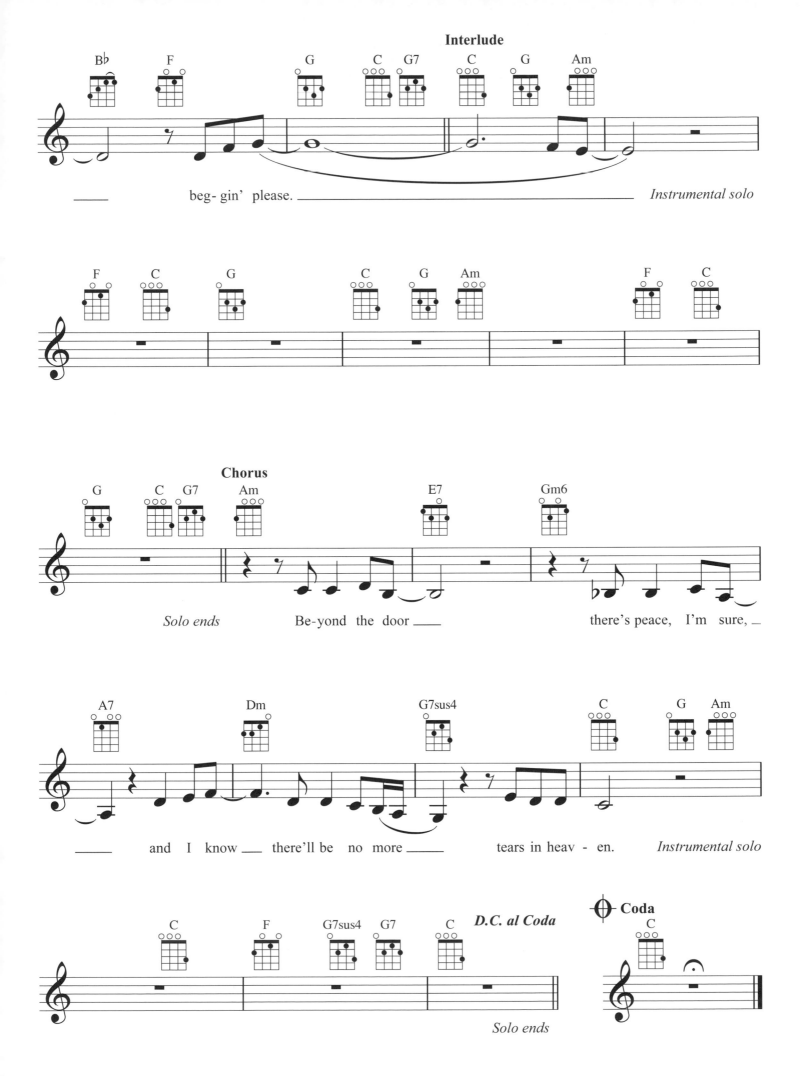

Interlude

_____ beg- gin' please. _____ *Instrumental solo*

Chorus

Solo ends   Be-yond the door _____   there's peace, I'm sure, _____

_____ and I know _____ there'll be no more _____ tears in heav - en.   *Instrumental solo*

D.C. al Coda   **Coda**

Solo ends

Layla

Words and Music by Eric Clapton and Jim Gordon

1. What will you do when you get lone - ly?
2., 3. *See additional lyrics*

No one wait - ing by your side.

You've been run - ning and hid - ing much too long.

You know it's just your fool - ish pride. Lay - la,

you've got me on my knees. Lay - la,

Copyright © 1970 by Eric Patrick Clapton
Copyright Renewed
International Copyright Secured   All Rights Reserved

Additional Lyrics

2. Tried to give you consolation,
   Your old man won't let you down.
   Like a fool, I fell in love with you.
   You turned my whole world upside down.

3. Make the best of the situation
   Before I fin'lly go insane.
   Please don't say we'll never find a way
   And tell me all my love's in vain.

My Father's Eyes

Words and Music by Eric Clapton

1. Sail - ing down   be - hind   the   sun,
2. Then the light   be - gins   to   shine
3. Then the jag - ged edge   ap - pears

wait - ing for ____ my   prince ____ to   come. ____
and   I   hear those an - cient   lull - a - bies. ____
         through the dis - tant   clouds ____ of   tears. ____

Pray - ing ____ for ____ the heal - ing rain
And   as ____ I watch this seed - ling grow,
And I'm like a bridge that ____ was washed a - way.

to re - store ____   my soul a - gain. ____
feel my heart start   to o - ver - flow. ____
My foun - da - tions   were made of clay. ____

Copyright © 1992 by E.C. Music Ltd.
International Copyright Secured   All Rights Reserved

When I look in ___
That's when I need ___ } my fa - ther's eyes, —
I looked in - to ___

(Look in - to ___ my fa - ther's eyes. ___

my fa - ther's eyes. ___

My fa - ther's eyes. ___

(Looked in - to ___ my fa -

My fa - ther's eyes. _____

- ther's eyes.) __

I looked in - to my __ fa - ther's eyes.
(Looked in - to my fa -

My fa - ther's eyes. _____

- ther's eyes.) __

Outro

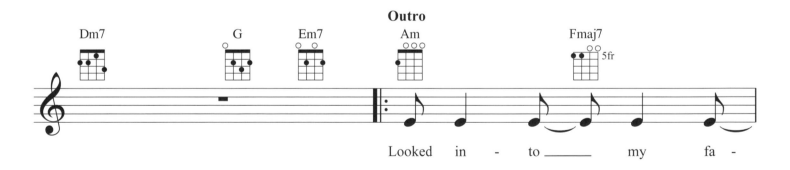

Looked in - to _____ my fa -

Repeat and fade

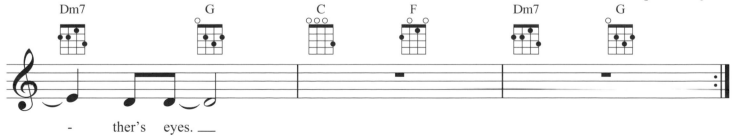

- ther's eyes. __

Nobody Knows You
When You're Down and Out
(Nobody Knows When You're Down and Out)
Words and Music by Jimmie Cox

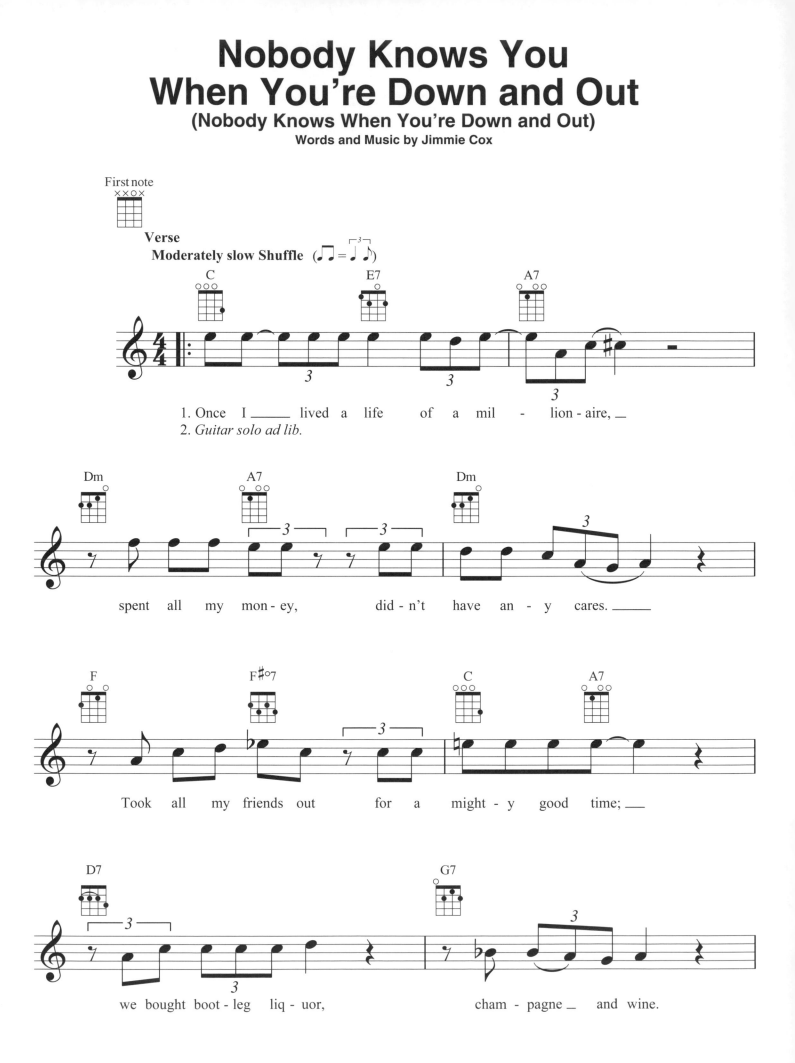

Copyright © 1923, 1929, 1950, 1959, 1963 UNIVERSAL MUSIC CORP.
Copyright Renewed
All Rights Reserved   Used by Permission

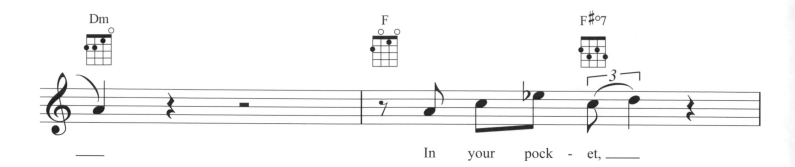

In your pock - et, ___

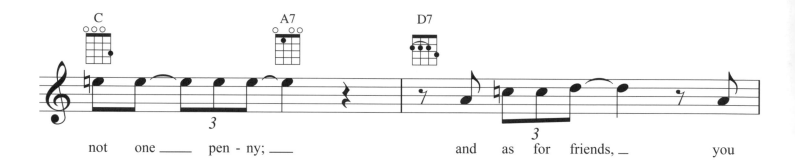

not one ___ pen - ny; ___ and as for friends, ___ you

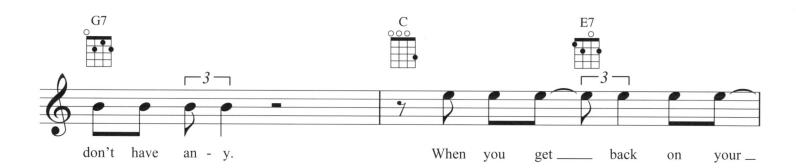

don't have an - y. When you get ___ back on your ___

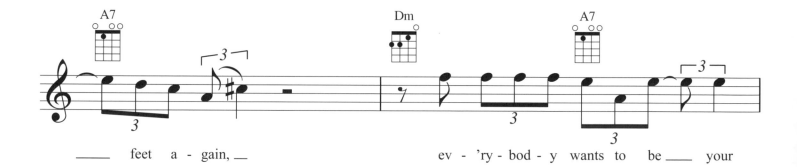

___ feet a - gain, ___ ev - 'ry - bod - y wants to be ___ your

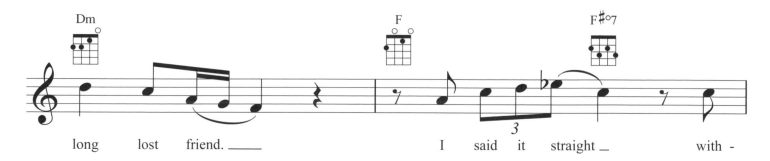

long lost friend. ___ I said it straight ___ with -

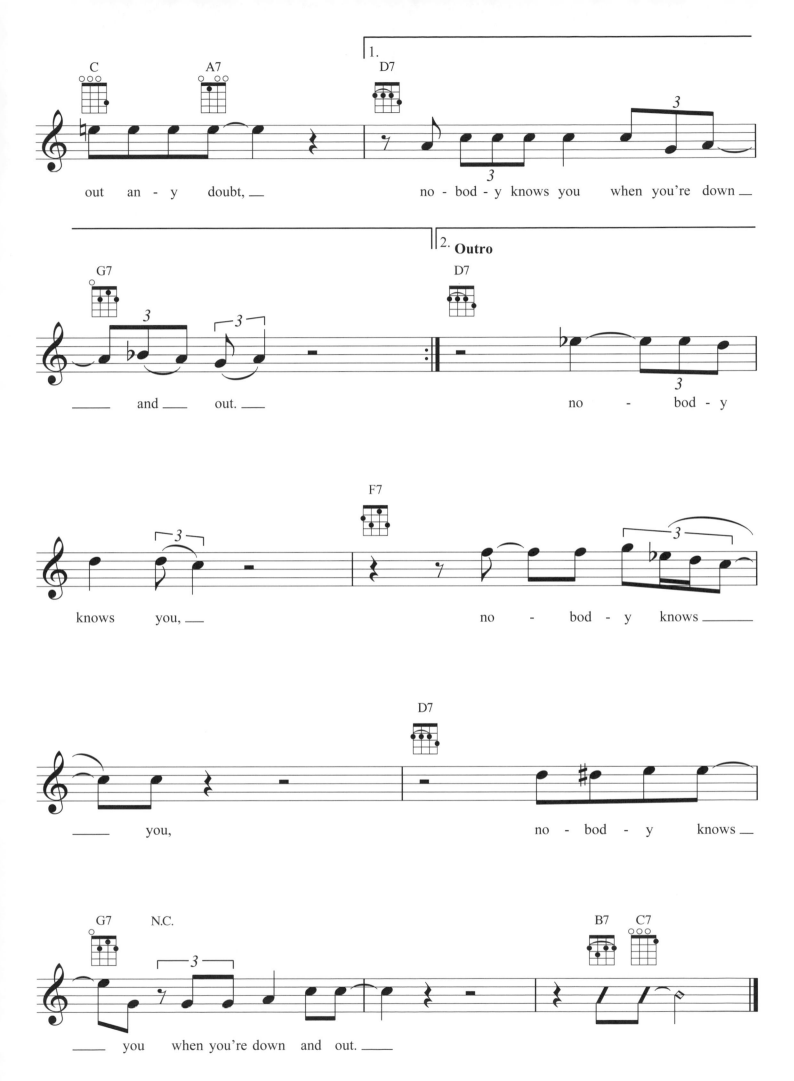

Pretending

Words and Music by Jerry Lynn Williams

Copyright © 1985, 1989 UNIVERSAL - SONGS OF POLYGRAM INTERNATIONAL, INC.,
UNIVERSAL MUSIC - CAREERS and STAGE THREE MUSIC LTD.
All Rights for STAGE THREE MUSIC LTD. Administered by STAGE THREE MUSIC (US) INC., A BMG CHRYSALIS COMPANY
All Rights Reserved Used by Permission

tryin' to get ___ the mu - sic ___ right. _____
sit - u - a - tions ___ change. ___
sad - ness ___ can't pre - vail. _____

Two _____ go ___ out ___ work - ing, ___ three stay home ___
You're nev - er who ___ you used to ___ think you are. How ___
Ev - 'ry - bod - y knows strong love ___ can't

To Coda ⊕

_____ at night. _____
strange.
fail.

Chorus 1

That's when she said she was ___ pre - tend - ing ___

just like she knew the plan. _____

That's when I knew ___ she was pre - tend - ing, ___ pre -

tend-ing to un - der-stand. _____ Pre - tend-ing, ___

pre - tend - ing, ___ pre -

tend - ing, ___

{ pre - tend - ing. ___
{ pre - tend - ing, ___ (pre - tend - ing, ___ pre -

Interlude

1.

2.

tend - ing.) ___ *Guitar solo - ad lib.*

D.S. al Coda

Coda

Chorus 2

Don't be pre - tend - ing ___

46

a - bout how you feel. _____   Don't be pre -

tend - ing _____   your love is   real.

Outro

1. Don't be pre -   2. Pre - tend - ing, _____

pre - tend - ing, _____   pre -

tend - ing, _____   pre -

tend - ing, _____ (pre - tend - ing,) _____ pre - tend - ing. _____

Running on Faith

Words and Music by Jerry Lynn Williams

Copyright © 1985 UNIVERSAL - SONGS OF POLYGRAM INTERNATIONAL, INC.,
UNIVERSAL MUSIC - CAREERS and STAGE THREE (CATALOGUES) LIMITED
All Rights for STAGE THREE MUSIC (CATALOGUES) LIMITED Administered by STAGE THREE MUSIC (US) INC.,
A BMG CHRYSALIS COMPANY
All Rights Reserved   Used by Permission

Pre-Chorus

I've ___ al - ways been

one to take each ___ and ev - 'ry day. ___

Seems like by now ___ I'd find a love who would

Chorus

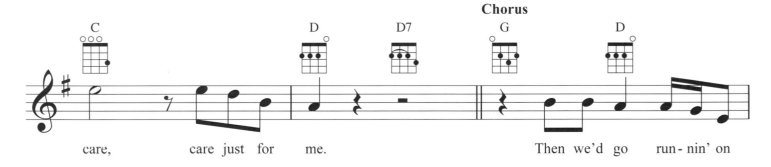

care, care just for me. Then we'd go run - nin' on

faith. All of our dreams ___ would come true. And our

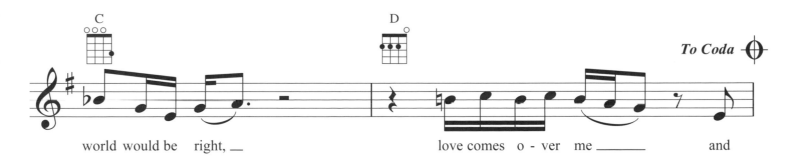

To Coda

world would be right, ___ love comes o - ver me ___ and

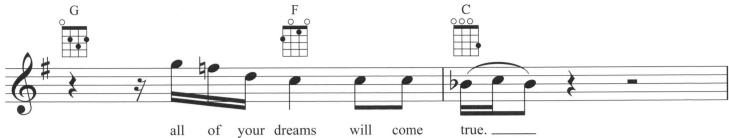

all of your dreams will come true. _____

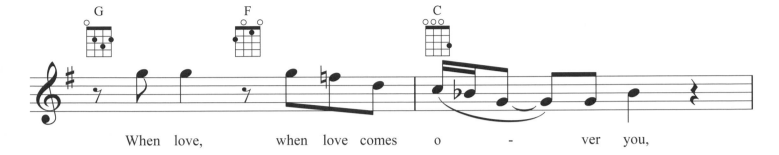

When love, when love comes o - ver you,

then all of your dreams _____ will come true.

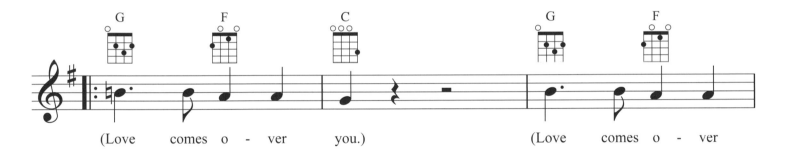

(Love comes o - ver you.) (Love comes o - ver

you.) Love comes, oh, o - ver you. _____

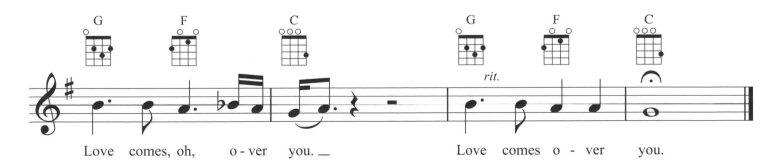

Love comes, oh, o - ver you. _ Love comes o - ver you.

Sunshine of Your Love

Words and Music by Eric Clapton, Jack Bruce and Pete Brown

First note

Verse
Moderate Rock

1. It's get - ting near dawn, ___ when
(2.) with you, my love. ___ The

lights close their tired ___ eyes. ___ I'll
light shin - ing through ___ on you. ___ Yes, I'm

soon be with you, ___ my ___ love, ___ to
with you, my love. ___ It's the

give you my dawn ___ sur - prise. ___ I'll
morn - ing and just ___ we ___ two. ___ I'll

be with you, dar - ling, soon. ___ I'll
stay with you, dar - ling, now. ___ I'll

Copyright © 1967, 1973 E.C. Music Ltd. and Dratleaf Music, Ltd.
Copyright Renewed
International Copyright Secured   All Rights Reserved

be with you when ___ the stars ___ start fall - ing.}
stay with you till ___ my seeds ___ are dried ___ up.}

(Instrumental)

Chorus

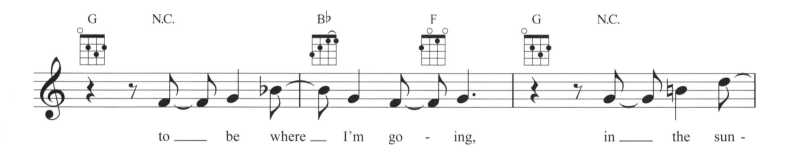

I've ___ been wait - ing so ___ long

to ___ be where ___ I'm go - ing, in ___ the sun -

- shine of ___ your love. _____

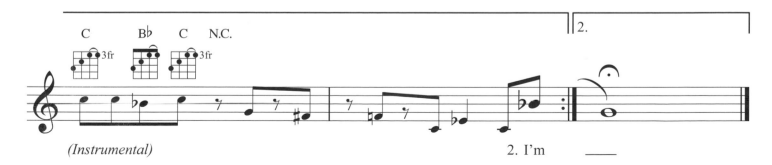

(Instrumental) 2. I'm ___

Wonderful Tonight

Words and Music by Eric Clapton

1. It's late in the eve - ning;
2. We go to a par - ty,
3. It's time to go home ___ now,

she's won-d'ring what clothes ___ to wear. ___ She puts on her make-
ev-'ry-one turns ___ to see ___ this beau-ti-ful la-
I've got an ach - ing head. ___ So I give her the car ___

- up and brush-es her long, ___ blonde hair. ___
- dy is walk-ing a - round ___ with me. ___
___ keys, and she helps me to bed. ___

And then she asks ___ me, "Do I look all right?" ___
And then she asks ___ me, "Do you feel all right?" ___
And then I tell ___ her, as I turn out the light, ___

Copyright © 1977 by Eric Patrick Clapton
Copyright Renewed
International Copyright Secured All Rights Reserved

just don't re - al - ize ____ how much ___ I love _____ you." *(Instrumental)*

D.C. al Coda

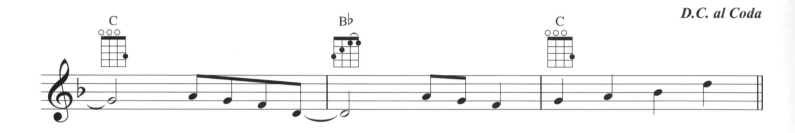

⊕ **Coda**   **Outro**

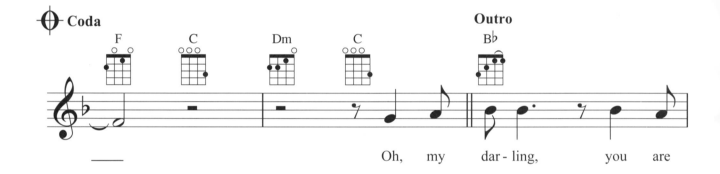

____   Oh,   my   dar - ling,   you   are

won - der - ful _____ to - night." ___   *(Instrumental)*